92
A

Robert Quackenbush

ARTHUR ASHE

AND HIS MATCH
WITH HISTORY

SIMON & SCHUSTER BOOKS FOR YOUNG READERS

SIMON & SCHUSTER BOOKS FOR YOUNG READERS
An imprint of Simon & Shuster Children's Publishing Division
1230 Avenue of the Americas, New York, New York 10020
Copyright © 1994 by Robert Quackenbush.
SIMON & SCHUSTER BOOKS FOR YOUNG READERS
is a trademark of Simon & Schuster
Manufactured in the United States of America

10 9 8 7 6 5 4 3 2

Library of Congress Cataloging-in-Publication Data
Quackenbush, Robert M. Arthur Ashe and his match with history /
Robert Quackenbush. p. cm. Summary: a biography of the
African American tennis champion who used his success
to work against the racial prejudice he had faced.
1. Ashe, Arthur—Juvenile literature. 2. Tennis players—
United States—Biography—Juvenile literature.
[1. Ashe, Arthur. 2. Tennis players. 3. Afro-Americans—
Biography.] I. Title. GV994.A7Q83 1993
796.342'092—dc20 [B] 93-14945 CIP

ISBN: 0–671–86597–8

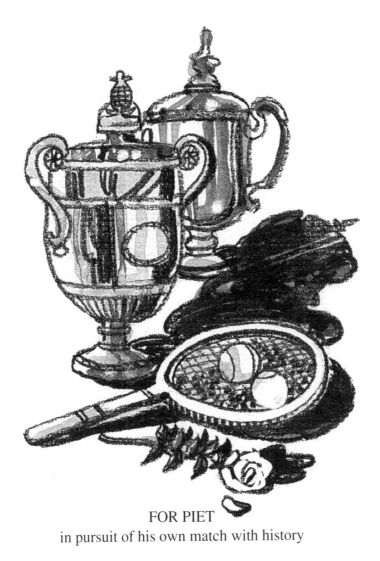

FOR PIET
in pursuit of his own match with history

ARTHUR GROWING UP IN RICHMOND, VIRGINIA

Arthur Robert Ashe, Jr., was born on July 10, 1943, in Richmond, Virginia, to Mattie Cunningham Ashe and Arthur Ashe, Sr. The family heritage was African American with a mixture of Sauk Indian and Mexican. Arthur's first American ancestor on his father's side was a nameless female slave who arrived in Virginia in 1735. She was one of millions of Africans who were brought to America and sold into bondage as cheap agricultural labor.

When Arthur was growing up, he learned the love of books and reading from his mother. He learned the importance of self-discipline and hard work from his father. Arthur's father supported the family by doing several jobs at the same time. He was chauffeur, gardener, and carpenter for several wealthy families in Richmond who were kind to the Ashes. But in Arthur's own words, he soon found out "that white people collectively did not really like black people." In those days Richmond, like other places in the Deep South, was a segregated city. By law African Americans could not attend the same schools or worship at the same churches as white people. Arthur learned to live with segregation. He attended an all-black school. He played in blacks-only parks. And when he took a No. 6 bus to his grandmother's house, he went to the back of the bus behind the white line.

THE LAST TIME ARTHUR SAW HIS MOTHER

When Arthur was four, his brother John was born. At around the same time, his father was hired as a special police officer to manage Richmond's largest park, the eighteen-acre Brookfield Park. With the post came a small, five-room frame house at 1610 Sledd Street, in the middle of the blacks-only playground. Arthur couldn't have been happier living in the new house. Nearby were baseball fields, an Olympic size swimming pool, and four tennis courts. Next to the house was a padlocked box filled with all kinds of sports equipment. And Arthur had the key! He liked sports, and he was good at them. He wasn't very big, but he was quick and fast.

When Arthur was six, tragedy struck. Mattie Ashe died suddenly following minor surgery. Arthur never forgot the last time he saw his mother alive. He was having breakfast one Saturday morning. He heard birds singing in a small oak tree outside. He saw his mother standing at the side door, wearing a blue corduroy bathrobe. His next memory was seeing her lifeless body lying in a coffin in the living room. A single red rose was placed in her hand. Roses had been his mother's favorite flower. After the funeral Mrs. Otis Berry, a patient, elderly widow, came to help raise the two boys.

11

ARTHUR BECOMES INTERESTED IN TENNIS.

Arthur's grandmother told him that his mother had gone to a better place. Arthur concluded that if he was a good boy and succeeded, he could be closer to his mother. He knew about success. He got straight A's at his school, Baker Elementary. More than that, his teachers drummed into the students that, despite white oppression, black people have always managed to find a way to succeed.

At age seven Arthur became interested in tennis. This might not have happened had he not come in contact with Ronald Charity, one of the nation's top black tennis players. Charity was a student at nearby Virginia Union University. He spent his summers working as a part-time tennis instructor at Brookfield Park. Arthur used to stand nearby and watch him practice. One day Charity came over to him and offered to teach him how to play the game. Arthur's fast reflexes made him a natural with a racket. By the time he was ten years old, he became known as "the kid who could play tennis." He was still small and thin, but he shocked a number of stronger and older youths when he won Brookfield's local tournament. Under Charity's watchful eyes, he kept improving his game by competing against grown-ups at the Richmond Racquet Club, a tennis club for black players.

DR. ROBERT JOHNSON, ARTHUR, AND ROBERT, JR.

In 1953 Charity introduced Arthur to Dr. Robert W. Johnson, a successful medical doctor in Lynchburg, Virginia. Dr. Johnson, an accomplished tennis player and teacher, promoted the game among young African Americans. Every summer he invited youngsters to his home. He and his son, Bobby, coached them and entered them in tournaments. One of Dr. Johnson's protégés was Althea Gibson, the first black player to win titles at England's Wimbledon tournament (the world's most coveted lawn tennis title) in 1957 and 1958. After seeing Arthur in action, Dr. Johnson wanted to work with him.

For eight summers Dr. Johnson coached Arthur. He stressed to Arthur the importance of good manners and composure on the courts. He believed that this would prevent racial problems as his young players entered the white tennis world. More than ever, it was a difficult world to enter. The United States Supreme Court ruled against segregation in 1954, but the ruling launched a national resistance to desegregation. Arthur was prevented from entering many tournaments in Virginia. He often had to play out of state. But wherever he went he sensed prejudice. Years later he told about his feelings during those days in his third autobiography, *Off the Court*. He said, "No player ever refused to appear on the court with me. No official ever called me a name. But the indirect rebuffs and innuendos left their scars."

15

TENNIS GREAT PANCHO GONZALES

Although Althea Gibson had paved the way for black players in the tennis world, Arthur did not really identify with her. He was looking for a male tennis hero to follow. When Arthur was about eleven years old, Charity took him to see his first pro match in Richmond. Richard ("Pancho") Gonzales, one of the greatest players of the day, was in the competition. Arthur saw that Gonzales had skin near the color of his own. He had found his idol. He wanted to be as great as Gonzales.

The following year Arthur's talent and determination earned him the rank of the best twelve-year-old player in the country. By the time Arthur was fourteen, Dr. Johnson was entering him in the National Junior Championships. At sixteen Arthur made his debut at the 1959 United States National Championships. At seventeen he won the American Tennis Association junior and men's titles. Arthur was the youngest champion ever at ATA, which was the black counterpart of the United States Lawn Tennis Association. As a new decade began, he was becoming the best young player since Althea Gibson. In order to keep climbing he had to be able to play winter tennis. But there were no winter games in Virginia. What could he do?

17

ARTHUR ASHE AT UCLA

Arthur's answer to the problem was to move to St. Louis, Missouri, and enroll at Sumner High School his senior year. He was invited to live with Richard Hudlin, a good friend of Dr. Johnson. Hudlin was a former captain of the University of Chicago tennis team. "The move was practical," wrote Arthur in *Off the Court*, "because each summer I had roamed farther and farther away from home. St. Louis would be the final break with Richmond."

Being away from Virginia that winter helped Ashe to develop a more powerful style. He shortened his backswing and added more wallop to his serve. In November 1960 he won his first USLTA national title, the National Juniors Indoors. Soon afterward he received a telephone call offering him a tennis scholarship to the University of California at Los Angeles. He gladly accepted the offer. He was the first black student to be given a scholarship by the University. After graduating from Sumner High with the highest grade point average in the class, he went on to California. He was now a tall and skinny (6'1", 152-pound) young man of eighteen years. He enrolled at UCLA as a student of business administration. In return for the scholarship, he was to put in 250 hours of work a year, mainly keeping the tennis courts tidy. He didn't mind working for his keep in order to receive a first-rate education and work with the country's best tennis coach, J. D. Morgan.

ASHE AND HIS NEW MENTORS AT UCLA

Two weeks after Ashe arrived at UCLA, his college tennis team was invited to play at Balboa Bay Club; but Ashe was not invited because of his color. Coach Morgan offered to halt the match, but Ashe stopped him. Ashe said that he did not want to start his college life with a protest over racial issues. The matter was closed. Ashe began his studies and entered other tournaments. He was surprised to find out that his childhood hero, Pancho Gonzales, lived a few blocks away from the UCLA campus. They practiced on the same courts. Gonzales gave him some playing tips. Soon Ashe's serve gained more sheer force than any other in the amateur game. He could send a ball slicing the court at 130 miles an hour.

In April 1963 Ashe was invited to play in an exhibition match at the California Club. "As we were leaving," Ashe says in *Off the Court*, "a gentle, well-dressed and very determined white woman came up to me." The lady was Mrs. Joan Ogner, the wife of an automobile dealer. She told him how much she enjoyed his game and asked what his plans were. Ashe said that if he had the money he would go to Wimbledon the following month. Mrs. Ogner asked him how much that would cost. Ashe said eight hundred dollars. Mrs. Ogner told him to stay put and left. In a few minutes she returned with the eight hundred dollars. To Ashe, Mrs. Ogner's generous act balanced the Balboa Bay Club incident.

21

DR. MARTIN LUTHER KING, JR.

Ashe lost in the third round at Wimbledon, but he gave a good display of his talent. He did the same at a tournament in Budapest, Hungary. Because of his strong performance overseas, Ashe was selected for the United States Davis Cup team, which played against teams from other nations.

In 1965 Ashe won the National Collegiate Athletic Association singles and doubles titles, making him the best college player in the United States. He also traveled with the United States Davis Cup team to New Zealand and Australia. He had become world famous. His picture appeared on the covers of *Life* and *Sports Illustrated*. He was paid to have his name put on tennis equipment and to endorse soft drinks.

That same year Dr. Martin Luther King, Jr., led a civil rights march in Selma, Alabama, as a protest against racial intolerance. Ashe used his fame to support the civil rights movement in the media and to help raise public awareness of racism in America. He told reporters how his color kept him out of tournaments as a boy in his hometown of Richmond, Virginia. On a hopeful note, he told *Sports Illustrated* about his travels with the United States Davis Cup team. "People in other countries read a lot about race troubles in the U.S.," he said. "But when they see two guys from the South like Cliff Richey and me, one white and one colored, both sharing a room and being close friends, it must do a little good."

THE FUNERAL OF DR. KING

During Ashe's last year at UCLA, his hometown, Richmond, declared February 4, 1966, Arthur Ashe Day. After his graduation from college at age twenty-three, Ashe served in the army for two years. When he fulfilled that obligation, he was a first lieutenant and the number two amateur tennis player in the nation. He aimed for the number one spot.

In 1968 Ashe won both the United States National and the United States Open singles titles. He was the only player ever to do so. He was launched to the number one spot. He went on to help the United States team win the Davis Cup from Australia. All of this happened at a low point in American history. In April Nobel Peace Prize-winner Dr. Martin Luther King, Jr., was assassinated. Ashe heard the shocking news on his car radio as he was driving over the George Washington Bridge in New York City. As soon as he crossed the bridge, he braked his car at the side of the road and sat stunned behind the steering wheel. Then in June came another shock: Robert F. Kennedy, who had fought for the Civil Rights Act of 1964, was assassinated. The tragic events of the times and the powerful emotions they induced in Ashe were reflected in his game. He played for all or nothing. During 1969, when amateurs and professionals began playing together for the first time, he was on a winning streak. He went for a two-month period without losing a match.

ASHE IN SOUTH AFRICA

In 1973 Ashe was the first black to be invited to compete in the South African Open. He felt challenged to accept. At the time no other country except Rhodesia (now called Zimbabwe) had laws that separated people by race. Ashe was familiar with that kind of injustice, having lived in the segregated South. He knew that he was invited because the South African government was trying to change its image in order to make the country eligible to be in the Olympic games. In spite of this Ashe agreed to go—but on his terms. First, he would not play before a racially segregated audience. Second, he would not come as an "honorary white," which meant denying his heritage. Third, he would be allowed to go wherever he pleased and say anything he wanted as though apartheid—the government's name for segregation—were not in effect. Surprisingly, the minister of immigration and sports agreed to his terms.

Ashe made it to the finals of the South African Open. But the main reason he went to South Africa was to show the oppressed children of the country a free black man in action. He went back many times to battle against apartheid. When freedom leader Nelson Mandela was released from prison after twenty-seven years, the first person he asked to visit during his tour of the United States was Arthur Ashe.

27

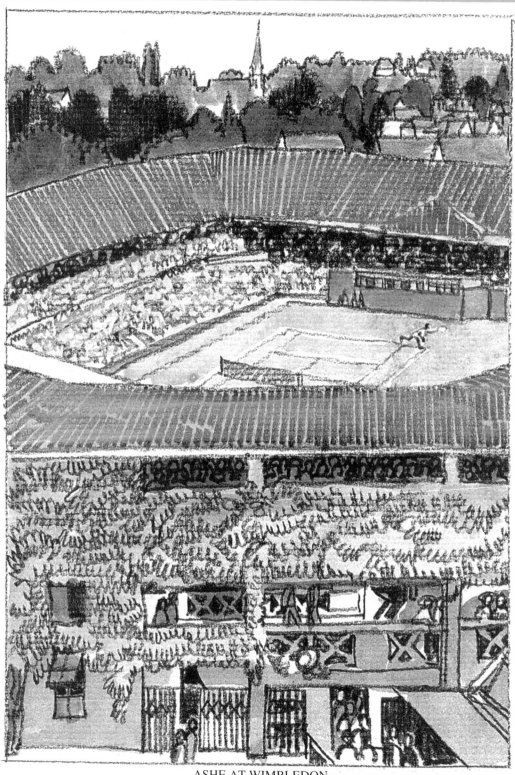

ASHE AT WIMBLEDON

By 1974 the tennis world was starting to ask if Ashe, at age thirty-one, had passed his peak. He had not won a major singles event since 1970, when he captured the Australian Open. He was now the fifth-ranked player in the United States, but he was determined to regain his title. He knew he could do it if he could win at the acclaimed World Championship Tennis Championships that spring in Dallas and at Wimbledon in 1975. He went to Puerto Rico for a tough training program. The training paid off. Ashe won in Dallas and collected the big prize—a solid gold tennis ball. Then he headed for England.

Ashe's opponent at Wimbledon was twenty-two-year-old Jimmy Connors, who, for the previous two years, had been taking the tennis world by storm. Ashe was determined to beat him. He discussed a game plan with a few of his friends and advisers. It was a radical change of strategy. Could he do it? Ashe knew that Connors was a very good counterpuncher. The harder his opponent hit a ball, the better Connors liked it. But Ashe did the opposite to confuse Connors. He sent Connors a lot of "junk"—balls that were the opposite of what Connors expected. He also forced Connors to the net so he could lob (loft the ball in an arc) over Connors' hard-hitting, two-handed backhand swing. His strategy worked. He won at Wimbledon and was once again the number one player in the world.

ASHE HAS HEART SURGERY.

Ashe went on to win five more tournaments in 1976. On October 14 of that year, he met photographer Jeanne Marie Moutoussamy of New York City. She was taking his photograph at a fund-raising benefit at the Felt Forum in New York. Arthur was impressed by her beauty, which was the blossoming of a mix of ancestries, including African American and East Indian. Jeanne was from Chicago and had attended the prestigious Cooper Union in New York. Ashe invited her to go to dinner with him the next evening. When he picked her up for their first date, he handed her a single rose—his mother's favorite flower. Four months later, on February 20, 1977, Arthur Ashe and Jeanne Marie Moutoussamy were married.

In July 1979 Ashe suffered a heart attack after returning from a strenuous overseas trip. He was told by heart specialists that he needed an operation, but he kept putting it off. His condition grew worse. In December, at age thirty-six, Ashe successfully underwent quadruple coronary bypass surgery. After that he was forbidden to play tennis. He was not discouraged. He knew he would always stay involved with tennis and sports. It was what he did best and what he felt most comfortable with. He continued to attend important tournaments and captained the United States Davis Cup team from 1981–1984. But his playing days were over.

ASHE BECOMES A MAN OF LETTERS.

Ashe moved on to new opportunities. He served as campaign chairperson of the American Heart Association and helped to educate the public about heart disease. He also devoted time to writing. Already he had co-authored two autobiographies, entitled *Advantage Ashe* (1967) and *Arthur Ashe:Portrait in Motion* (1976). In addition, he had contributed to an instructional tennis book called *Mastering Your Tennis Strokes* (1976). Starting fresh, he set to work to produce an instructional tennis book of his own called *Arthur Ashe's Tennis Clinic* (1981). At the same time he co-authored his third autobiography, entitled *Off the Court* (1981). It was in his character to find a way to turn adversity into something positive.

Ashe had another coronary bypass operation in 1983. Then he went right back to work. He received more honors. In 1985 he was inducted into the National Lawn Tennis Hall of Fame. In 1988 he saw the publication of his greatest work, entitled *A Hard Road to Glory*. This three-volume history of the black American athlete took him five years to complete. In the meantime, his outstanding career earned him honorary doctorates from Dartmouth College, LeMoyne-Owen College, Princeton University, Saint John's University, and Virginia Union University. To top it all, he became a father in 1987, when Jeanne Moutoussamy-Ashe gave birth to their daughter, Camera.

ASHE WITH HIS WIFE AND DAUGHTER

Throughout his life, Arthur Ashe had faced challenges posed by a difficult period in America's history. In the 1940s he was a young African American striving to find his place in the sun in the segregated South. In the 1950s, during national resistance to desegregation, he found a spot for himself in the white-ruled tennis world. In the 1960s and 1970s he used his many tennis achievements to give a voice to the fight against discrimination all over the world. Then, in the 1980s, when the nation's number one health threat was heart disease, Ashe again stepped forward. As a survivor of two heart operations, he became a spokesperson for the American Heart Association.

In the 1990s Arthur Ashe became engaged in still another national struggle—the defeat of AIDS. In 1988 he discovered he had the dread virus. He and his doctors believed he had become infected through a tainted blood transfusion during one of his coronary bypass operations. (The nation's blood bank was not purified of the virus until 1985.) He went public with the news in April 1992. The following June he told *People* magazine, "You're not going to believe this, but living with AIDS is not the greatest burden I've had in my life. Being black is." Shortly afterward, he began a new match with history. He founded the Arthur Ashe Foundation for the Defeat of AIDS.

EPILOGUE

Arthur Ashe died on February 7, 1993, at age forty-nine, of pneumonia, a complication of AIDS. He was buried next to his mother in his hometown of Richmond, Virginia. He was mourned not only by the tennis community, but by civil rights activists and statesmen around the world. A total of eleven thousand people attended his funeral in Richmond and his memorial service in New York City.

From an early age Ashe was involved in a match with history. Consequently, his life became a series of spectacular breakthroughs. His athletic achievements alone qualify him as a legend. He was the first African American male athlete to break down barriers in the traditionally white world of tennis. He was the first black player to win the United States Open and Wimbledon. Later he used his personal struggles to help others as national chairperson of the American Heart Association and as founder of the Arthur Ashe Foundation for the Defeat of AIDS. A devoted husband and father, he also gave freely of his time to help young people enter the world of tennis. For many boys and girls he was the first person to give them a tennis lesson. Through it all, he continued to work as a commentator for ABC Sports and HBO and to write a column for the *Washington Post*. His accomplishments inspire people everywhere—young and old alike—who strive for success against impossible odds.

FURTHER READING

Books:

Ashe, Arthur, with Neil Amdur. *Off the Court.* New York: New American Library, 1981.

Ashe, Arthur, with Frank Deford. *Arthur Ashe: Portrait in Motion.* Boston: Houghton Mifflin, 1975.

Ashe, Arthur, and Clifford Gewecke, Jr. *Advantage Ashe.* New York: Coward-McCann, Inc., 1967.

Magazines:

People, June 8, 1992.
Sports Illustrated, September 20, 1965; August 29, 1966.

Newspapers:

The New York Times, February 8, 1993. By-line: Lawrence K. Altman.

Other Books in this Series:

CLEAR THE COW PASTURE,
I'M COMING IN FOR A LANDING!
A Story of Amelia Earhart

DON'T YOU DARE SHOOT THAT BEAR!
A Story of Theodore Roosevelt

MARK TWAIN?
WHAT KIND OF NAME IS THAT?
A Story of Samuel Langhorn Clemens

OLD SILVER LEG TAKES OVER!
A Story of Peter Stuyvesant

QUIT PULLING MY LEG!
A Story of Davy Crockett

STOP THE PRESSES,
NELLIE'S GOT A SCOOP!
A Story of Nellie Bly

WHO LET MUDDY BOOTS INTO
THE WHITE HOUSE?
A Story of Andrew Jackson